RED CLOUD

RED CLOUD

By Ed McGaa

DILLON PRESS

MINNEAPOLIS, MINNESOTA

Dillon Press, Inc., 500 South Third Street
Minneapolis, Minnesota 55415

Printed in the United States of America

Library of Congress Cataloging in Publication Data

McGaa, Ed.
  Red Cloud.

  (The Story of an American Indian)
  SUMMARY: A biography of the Oglala Indian who rose
to leadership in the Sioux nation because of his skill with
weapons and words.
  1. Red Cloud, Sioux chief, 1822-1909—Juvenile literature.
2. Oglala Indians—Biography—Juvenile literature. [1. Red
Cloud, Sioux chief, 1822-1909. 2. Oglala Indians—Biography.
3. Indians of North America—Biography]   I. Title.
E99.03R375   970'.004'97   77-12662
ISBN 0-87518-151-1

ON THE COVER:
Red Cloud in about 1890.
Smithsonian Office of Anthropology,
Bureau of American Ethnology Collection

RED CLOUD

Red Cloud was a great leader of the Lakota during the years when the Indian people were losing their land to the white people moving west.

In the Lakota language, the name Lakota means an alliance of friends. Red Cloud was certainly a friend to his people as he battled the white people, first with weapons and then with words.

The Lakota people are also called Sioux. The name Sioux is a French variation of an Ojibway or Chippewa word that means enemies. To those who would harm his people, Red Cloud was indeed an enemy—but also a man who earned the respect of his enemies by his courage, honesty, and dignity.

Red Cloud died in his South Dakota home in 1909, at the age of eighty-seven.

Contents

Sioux camp at Pine Ridge Agency, 1890.
South Dakota State Historical Society.

CHAPTER I

Circle of His People

The drums were beating like the heartbeat of a happy people. The Lakota, or Sioux, were leaving their tipis and joining the moving circle of dancers. Young Mahpiya Luta, Red Cloud, watched them. He thought the whole world must move in this circle of his people.

The tipis of his sisters in the camp of Old Smoke were all in the circle. Red Cloud had been young when his father, a Brule Sioux chief, died. His mother had been raised by Old Smoke, an Oglala Sioux chief, so he took her children into his camp, also. When his mother died, Red Cloud was raised by his sisters.

To Red Cloud it seemed that the moving circle of people dancing were all his family and he was part of them.

Around and around went the people. The men and boys danced in a fast step that tested their strong muscles. The women danced in a quiet bounce, making the pretty seeds and tassels they wore sway in a beautiful way.

Red Cloud watched his people go around that circle in times of pain. He saw his people go around that circle in times of joy. The old ones told Red Cloud that pain and joy have their place on the circle. Sometimes he would be at the joy place on the circle and sometimes at the pain place. The old ones said both joy and pain made a man a man and a woman a woman, and in time the circle would move to both places.

The old ones told Red Cloud many things as he sat with them. He liked to listen to them and watch them. So quickly they could slice the buffalo into thin strips. Then they hung the strips outdoors to dry so the meat would not spoil. This went on all over the camp after the men had been hunting. And when one tipi had meat, all tipis had meat. Even the tipis of those too old to hunt, or those who had no man to hunt for them. There were no poor or no rich, all were well off. If you could hunt well and could give much meat to those who needed it, you had earned honor.

And sometimes Red Cloud would watch the older ones grind the wild plums, cherries, and other berries that the women had gathered and dried.

Yes, as the older ones worked, they said that pain and joy come in a circle. Red Cloud was to learn in his eighty-seven years how true this is. The joy of growing up with his free and well fed and friendly people was to move around the circle to the pain of his grown-up years.

Red Cloud was born on the rolling prairie land between the Black Hills and the Missouri River. His people were hunting the buffalo which roamed what is now South Dakota and Nebraska. But the people of Red Cloud, the Lakota or Sioux, were being crowded from all sides. At the time Red Cloud was born, about 1822, the fight for land was on.

From his cradle board, sometimes on his mother's back and sometimes hung in the tipi or on a tree, Red Cloud could see and learn from the beginning of his life. He saw endless prairie and the cool, clear rivers the Lakota camped beside. He could see the faraway herds of buffalo as his people moved from one camp to another.

Long ago, the old ones said, his people had lived in the East. They had lived near the ocean where they hunted, fished, and learned of all that was hidden in Mother Earth. They learned of her fruits. And they learned of the good herbs, roots, stems, and leaves. These are now called vegetables and medicines. Many of Mother Earth's gifts had not been known to the non-Indian people before the Indians showed them to the early white settlers. A few of these gifts which the many different Indian people and Mother Earth gave to the world are corn, potatoes, tomatoes, pumpkins, squashes, lima beans, strawberries, and tobacco.

But as more white settlers came, Red Cloud's ancestors had moved west. His people called themselves the Lakota, one of the Seven Council Fires of Friendly People.

It was while they lived in what is now Minnesota (*Minne-ota,* much water) that the Lakota had to learn to live in a different way. It was about 1600, and other tribes had been pushed west by the non-Indians. The hunting, fishing and growing they could do on the ocean and near the rivers and lakes could not be done on the prairies further west.

So they had to become hunters of the roaming herds of buffalo, elk, and other animals which were brothers and gave life to the people. The Indian would not kill these brothers if the people were not hungry. When he did kill for food, the Indian would say a prayer of gratitude to the brother who gave life to the people. "Forgive me brother, but my people must live!" was the quick prayer spoken as the Sioux hunter drove his horse in beside the running buffalo to send his lance or arrow through *Tatanka* — the buffalo.

As more and more land was taken from the Indians by the non-Indians, there were fewer herds to hunt on less and less land. So when the men would fight other tribes for what space was left, it was not easy for anyone; the children did not know if their fathers would return. Always being on the move was something new, and if the Lakota people had been less brave or less able to change to new ways there would be no Lakota alive today.

By the time Red Cloud was born, his people had learned the new hunter-warrior ways very well. For they were a brave and strong and smart people. They knew how to adapt to changing conditions in order to survive, yet they would not give up the deep beauty of the old values which were proven through the trial of time.

Those times when Red Cloud was a young boy are hard to understand for many non-Indians. The times were also very hard to understand even for Red Cloud and his people, who were living then.

For many thousand years there had been land enough for everyone. Oh yes, at times one tribe would disagree with another, as one of us might disagree about who should have the extra piece of meat. Which of us has never fought with our brother or sister? Tribes had skirmishes and disputes, too, but nothing to compare to the world wars of Europe and the endless attempts of nations to destroy other nations. No North American Indian leader or prophet ever attempted to conquer all other tribes. In comparison to Europeans, the Indian people were extremely peaceful. They did not try to conquer the whole world for themselves as did the armies of Europe, one after the other.

The Indian people had a different idea about owning land that kept them from getting involved in terrible national wars. The people knew that they were put here by the Great Spirit, and that Mother Earth was to be respected because she too was put here for the Great Spirit's children. Most of all, the people did not believe they had to have treasures, possessions, or land to be wealthy and this was why the powerful Indian tribes did not have major wars with each other.

Mother Earth was big and she had so many good things that she taught the Lakota and other Indian people to trust her, and to share her.

Probably no other people have looked as deeply into Mother Earth as the Indian people. While other people were building bridges and inventing machines, the Indian people were learning to be a part of all that is. Mother Earth, Father Sky, and all that is holy in the four directions. There was truth to learn from all.

But now white people came rushing in. It seemed that they did not see the ways of Mother Earth. Or the big vision. They came from crowded cities across the ocean; dissatisfied, they left their European culture to board boats and cross an ocean — to build crowded cities on this side of the ocean. They kept what they found for themselves and pushed the Indian people inland.

More and more came. They seemed to see only themselves. They seemed to see only today. When they had crowded tribe against tribe, they wanted even that land.

It is at this point that Red Cloud was born. Many Indian tribes were fighting for survival and the few buffalo herds that were left.

They had learned from the circle of joy and pain that they must not feel sorry for themselves, or let their people die mourning what was gone. They had to look ahead and do what must be done — "so that the people will live."

For this reason Red Cloud learned to do the brave thing without running away. For this reason Red Cloud learned to do what was right for the people, not just for himself.

No one could tell Red Cloud what to do — he was free to decide. And he would not tell others what to do. But decisions must be "so that the people will live." An Indian boy was always taught that he must live for the good or well-being of his people, tribe, or of his nation. He must always place the welfare or interests of the group above his own interests, and not be selfish.

So Red Cloud learned not to get glory for himself, but to care for his brothers and sisters.

He learned not to misuse Mother Earth. Her growing ones, all the plants and animals, were related to him as brothers and sisters. He must accept from them and give of himself as they did.

He learned not to be well fed if others in the circle were hungry.

As a boy Red Cloud learned to hunt to feed the people. And to use the hides from the buffalo and deer for warm clothing, warm tipis, and warm robes for cold winter nights. The birds also provided food. So close did Red Cloud and his people feel to brother bird that they wore colorful feathers as part of their clothing.

Trees and rocks, bird and animal, all had beautiful things to teach each other, all children of Mother Earth.

But Red Cloud was barely out of the cradle board on his

Sioux camp, from copyrighted photo 1907 by E. Curtis.
Minneapolis Public Library Athenaeum.

mother's back when the black clouds of forts and wagon roads began to darken the skies of his people. The Lakota had been pushed to what is now western South Dakota and Nebraska, and eastern Colorado, Wyoming and Montana.

Red Cloud was barely able to see the endless prairies before they started closing in on him.

He was barely able to see the herds of buffalo before they and their brothers, the Lakota, entered a place on the circle so painful it seemed it would never move on to joy.

For now Red Cloud and his people would be pushed no further. They defended their homeland.

CHAPTER II

Brave
Stand

The brave Lakota had fought many tribes to live on this land. Now the white army began to put a road right through the middle of it.

So Red Cloud and his people fought the white army. *"Hupo-hupo-hokahey,"* Red Cloud's stirring cry would ring. "Come on, come on brothers. Let's go." And fearlessly they fought to preserve the dignity and beauty of their Indian way. Later another great Oglala leader, Crazy Horse, would also emerge and his cry would echo Red Cloud's: *"Hokahey* brothers, come with me into battle for it is a good day to die!"

Red Cloud had learned well the horsemanship for which his people were famous. He and his horse became as one.

He had learned well the warrior ways. His bow and arrow had strength behind them now and he faced his people's enemies with skill. Now Red Cloud also captured and learned to fire the new guns that he must use to fight the white army and its endless stream of supplies.

He and other wise leaders saw that they must close the road that cut through Lakota hunting grounds. This road they must close was called the Bozeman Trail.

It was the year 1866. Red Cloud was in his forties. It was the mid-point in his life.

He and the other brave Lakotas did a very hard thing; they fought even through the winter. This had not been done before very often. Bad blizzards could come suddenly. Man and horse could starve. Tracks could be followed. And this all was added to the death lying in front of the cannons and rifles of the white armies.

But skill and bravery paid off at such battles as that of the defeat of Captain Fetterman and his troops at Fort Philip Kearney (Wyoming).

In such battles the Lakota earned hard-won victories over the whites. They were competing against a people who had used the war machinery for centuries.

In precious little time, Red Cloud's people had learned that the bow and arrows and coup sticks were no match in combat with cannons that could mow down castles and fortress walls. A circle of tipis was small business for cannons and heavy artillery.

The Indian women and children were never far behind their men as they fought against hardened soldiers who had been away from home and family much of their lives fighting battles.

As we look back, it seems odd that many history books have turned the story around. Who had the savage ways?

Although many of the white enemies Red Cloud and his people fought against were professional killers, Red Cloud and the camps knew victory. Toward the end of 1867, the leaders of the white people saw that Red Cloud was leading several thousand brave fighters. Red Cloud's warriors killed five soldiers for every warrior that they lost due to their expert horsemanship, especially in hand-to-hand combat with the mounted white cavalry. The tough training since a very young age now paid off for the fearless Sioux warriors.

Either a flood of white troops must be sent to fight a long and high-priced war, or the whites must give in to Red Cloud. The white army was losing face in Washington after boasting how easily the Lakota could be destroyed.

Red Cloud said that the forts of the whites must be closed. The Bozeman Trail must be closed. The white men must leave the Lakota's hunting grounds.

Red Cloud and his brave people had won. The Treaty of 1868 was won by the brave stand of the Sioux people under Red Cloud's leadership. The government in Washington gave in. Only when Fort Laramie was destroyed by the Army would Red Cloud sign the treaty which promised to leave all of western South Dakota to the Sioux nation forever. "For as long as grass will grow and rivers flow and as long as the dead lie buried, this area will belong to the Sioux nation. No portion of this land shall be ceded except by three-fourths of the adult males signatures of the entire Sioux nation."

Young Red Cloud had been taught the ways of a warrior; he had been ready to defend his people against this white army. But now he had to learn to defend his people against the white's dishonest treaties. The white people did not honor the treaty of 1868.

Red Cloud had been taught by the old ones that all of life is part of him, that the Great Spirit is an ever-present relative to him. So his words must flow as straight as the straight stem of the holy pipe. The others would know if he did not tell the truth. Surely the Great Spirit would know.

But these white people seemed to walk alone. They did not know the Great Spirit. Their vision held just themselves and their lifetime. So they tried to buy land and buy Indian leaders with presents and with promises.

But Indian leaders — Lakota leaders — did only as their people decided. Decisions were made by all, not one. And when a people, through their leader, would not sign, the white people forced a few captive chiefs to sign treaties ceding land to the United States government. Never did the government honor the three-fourths signature clause of the treaty of 1868 that the Sioux had won through combat. Land promised the Indians for "as long as the rivers flow" was taken away when white people looked at it and wanted it.

And yet the white people laughed at the Indian people for accepting gifts today that would mean starvation tomorrow. They did not stop to look at a Mother Earth that restocked herself for those who lived by her laws. A Mother Earth that takes care of those who take only what they need.

So were the times in which Red Cloud became *Itanca*, leader. A leader must carry out the will of his people and his cares must be for them, not for himself. This was all a part of Red Cloud's training from the time he first began to look around Old Smoke's camp.

Though he was an Oglala Sioux chief, Old Smoke did not put his tipi in the center of the circle. It was part of all the circle. Joined with all the other parts.

Only during the annual sacred ceremony, the Sun Dance held in late summer, was the center of the circle occupied. The Sun Dance was taught by the Great Spirit through his

Red Cloud (on right) and American Horse in 1891 photo by Grabill.
From the collections of the Library of Congress.

No. 3691. "Red Cloud and American Horse."
The two most noted Chiefs now living. Photo and
copyright '91 by Grabill, P. & V. Co., Deadwood.

daughter, the Buffalo Calf Maiden, whom he sent down to the Lakota people. It was held every year in late summer to thank the Great Spirit for all that he had given the people.

A sacred tree (cottonwood) was cut and brought to the center of an arena. The sacred tree was placed in the place of honor in the center. There all would see its limbs raised from Mother Earth to Father Sky and to the west, north, east and south, for all is holy. From above *Tunkahshilah*, God, looked down on his family and children.

To be Lakota and a great one was *not* to have a storeroom full of valuables on valuable land. To be Lakota and a great one was *not* to have a bigger house in the center of all the others. To be Lakota and a great one *was* to give away meat and presents after a hunt. To live bravely "so that the people will live."

Perhaps at the time of Red Cloud this was even more important than at anytime in his people's history. For now he must keep them alive in order to keep their values alive.

Always looming around the life of Red Cloud was that closing-in circle of Indian land. This closing-in circle grew smaller and smaller as the land on which white people would never enter was entered. Troops sent to protect Indian rights bowed on signal to the whites who wanted ever more land.

Treaty.

It is a simple word. It is even a small word. But in the hands of a people who see only themselves it is a big word bent on destroying. Could the Lakota come through the test alive and still be Lakota?

To the invading whites, the Indians, or at least their ways, must be destroyed. Their old roving way of life was in the way of the farmers and ranchers. Those Indians left alive must give up their Indian ways and become farmers and ranchers also.

The treaty of 1868 promised the Lakota all of western South Dakota and parts of North Dakota (and Nebraska hunting rights). The treaty stated: "This land, all of western South Dakota and the Black Hills (*Paha Sapa*) will belong to the Sioux for as long as the grass will grow, as long as the rivers will flow and as long as the dead lie buried. This is forever."

For giving up their other land, the Lakota were promised schools, food, clothing, and other supplies.

Red Cloud and other wise leaders would not sign until the troops were out and the forts left empty. They even waited two months to make sure the Army would not come back. Then, November 6, 1868, Red Cloud went to Fort Laramie to sign.

The "other supplies" the Lakota were promised included tools meant to make the Lakota into farmers. White people promised the government they would force farming on the Lakota in four years. This was a vow made by people back east who did not understand freedom. Freedom to the Lakota means living as you choose to live, and as is good for all the people.

When Indian children are very small they begin to decide for themselves what to do. They learn to do what is right for all the people, not just for themselves. Red Cloud was taught as a very young child not to cry out because he could give the whole circle of his people away to the enemy.

From the time he was small he was taught by wise leaders and teachers who put him forth in Mother Nature's testing ground. He learned to make decisions but always he had examples to look up to. Red Cloud's family respected what was in him and what caused him to decide as he did. And Red Cloud learned to respect others and would never force them to do something that he could not do himself.

The Lakota were very disgusted at the ignorance of the white people who came from the east to force their ways off on other people.

They knew *Wakan Tanka* (the Great Spirit) and Mother Earth do not work this way. They respect each piece of life and let it work its way up in its own time and its own new and different way.

In another day the Lakota probably would have pitied these people who knew so little of the holy ways. But it was hard to pity a people who rushed about ordering others around. It was hard to teach a people who would not be quiet and learn. A people who used cannons and rifles and armies against those who might have shared so much with them.

The time came when Red Cloud spoke sharply to these people from the east who would force his people to plant crops on soil that was continually a victim of drought and grasshopper plagues. Those who did give in and try to farm had their crops burned or eaten on this land that the white people had not wanted.

But now, as the Treaty of 1868 was being signed, the people from the east were very quiet about the farming clause of the treaty. They knew the Lakota would not like it.

As it turned out, treaties were another weapon like guns and cannons. Later the treaties were forgotten if white people wanted the land that had been deeded to the Indians. Or they would throw back a clause or two at the Indian people to get more land on the grounds that the Indian people would not farm the land. Yet countless white farmers could not grow crops on the poor land with little rainfall.

It had been one thing for Red Cloud to learn to be a good warrior to defend his people against white people's cannons and guns. Now he must learn to defend his people against their treaties.

He was learning quickly.

He and other wise chiefs would not sign the Treaty of 1868 until the troops were out and the forts abandoned. Remember, he even waited two months to make sure the Army would not come back.

But after signing the treaty, Red Cloud never again went into battle against the white army because he had given his word that he would not fight again. Many times, though, he had to use his sharp mind in battle with the leaders of the white people. For they forgot their promises.

CHAPTER III

By Wit
and Word

In 1870, Red Cloud and other Lakota leaders went to the big city, Washington, D. C., where the white leaders lived.

The train trip east was something very new to people who had lived close to Mother Earth. Big train engines and clattery bridges and one big city after another would have frightened some people who had not seen any of it before. And now Red Cloud and those with him were seeing it all at once.

But an Indian who is truly united with Mother Earth and all that is does not scare easily. And a leader who has united his life to that of his people cannot lose his composure. His people will be hungry and cold if he shows any weakness to this Great White Father, the President, back east.

Red Cloud found that this was a "white father" who was under pressure from his people to take the land of Red Cloud's people. The white people who wanted the Indian land wanted the Indian people to give it up quickly. So they hoped to frighten the Lakota leaders by showing them many big buildings and big cities and great numbers of people. They even had a Marine parade and a show of arms to demonstrate the power of the white armies.

A close-up view of the Black Hills.
South Dakota State Historical Society.

The white people hoped the Lakota would take the left-over land without saying a word. They did not know the proud Lakota.

Red Cloud had been willing to give his life in battle to defend the good life of his people. Now he had vowed not to go to war, and he kept his word. But now he would give his life in a battle of words and wits to keep his people and their ways alive.

What a strange place for this first big skirmish of the new battle — Washington, D. C. Red Cloud had left his people in the circle of tipis on their homeland which got smaller every year.

Red Cloud now looked at Washington, D. C. He saw that the white man's cities are not built around the circle of the people. They are built in squares.

Red Cloud thought of the Lakota leaders who never took the center of the circle for themselves. *Itanca,* or leader, was a part of the circle, a part of the people. Red Cloud saw no circle of a people all part of one another here. No, he saw one square of people after another.

Some of the squares that people lived in had big, beautiful houses. Some of the squares had poor, run-down houses. And right in the middle of these houses was a really big house. This is where the leader of the white people lives, Red Cloud was told. He was expected to be very impressed, but he would wait and decide for himself.

This also was something new, to see a big house of an important man living in the middle of the people who had less than he had. The only one who lived in the center of the circle of the Lakota was the holy tree during the days of the Sun Dance.

During these days the holy tree would call the people around it back to Mother Earth, Father Sky, and all that is above. The four colors tied to the tree would call the people to be part of all that is holy in the four directions. The four colors were red, white, black, and yellow which also stood for the four races of man, holy colors because the Great Spirit made the four races. The Indian people were not a prejudiced people; they freely took in the brave black people who ran away from the cruel slave plantations. The black people were adopted into the tribes as brothers. Kee-awk-sah-sapa was a very famous black Lakota who was adopted by the Oglalas.

And the dancers would join themselves to the tree to be part of the life she stood for. They would tie strips of raw-hide to their flesh and to the tree. And the dancers and the tree became one in a pulsing, living dance before all.

The dancers would pray their own prayer. They would give thanks and give their participation in their own way. But each prayer would be their way of praying the Sun Dance prayer.

"Wakan Tanka (Great Spirit)
Have mercy on me
I want to Live (part of all)
So this I do."

Perhaps the dancer's child had nearly died and his life had been spared.

Perhaps the dancers were about to do a hard thing, and needed courage.

First, in the Sun Dance they would become part of all that is. Then they would receive strength from the powers of all that is. And in gratitude, they gave their lives to the people.

Red Cloud thought of all this as he looked at these people who were so proud of their cities and bridges and cannons. Their churches were even big buildings to show off.

But in Washington, D. C., Red Cloud saw no simple holy tree that called people back to Mother Earth, Father Sky, and all that has power and is holy in every direction.

No. He saw a big square building in the middle of many square blocks that made up the city. This building stuck out from the rest, it was so rich. The "biggest man in the country" lived there, Red Cloud was told. But he waited to make up his own mind. When Red Cloud did see him he looked deep into this man, the "Great White Father," President Ulysses S. Grant.

Red Cloud saw all the fine things this man had. Red Cloud had also seen that not far from where this man lived were people who had none of these riches. He saw white people and black people whose faces were thin and hungry just like the faces of his own cold, sick, and hungry people. For now his people had no buffalo for homes and food. And his people had gotten new diseases from the white people. The Holy Men had known how to cure the illnesses of the Lakota. In Mother Earth were the medicines they needed. But now the children were dying from strange diseases the white men brought.

The food sent to Red Cloud's people was low-grade and it was white food. Red Cloud's people did not know how to fix it nor did they like it as well as they had liked the plentiful bounty of Mother Earth's fruits, vegetables, and meats.

So Red Cloud looked at the hungry white and black people. And he looked at the "Great White Father." He looked at him as his people look at their leaders — deep inside. Only if a heart sorrows in face of hunger, and a person gives away his things, and his life, for them, is he great.

So Red Cloud spoke. With the deep talk of a man for his people, he told of the new life that was killing his people like sheep. He told of the men the Great White Father sent to look after the supplies meant for the Lakota. He spoke of those agents who "filled their own pockets."

Very clearly, Red Cloud spoke.

But these people who lived in their rich squares did not hear very well. So for the next thirty-nine years Red Cloud would hear himself saying the same things over and over and over. And for the next thirty-nine years, he would hear words like "move to Indian Territory" (Oklahoma) and other threats.

There is a circle of joy and pain, the old ones had told Red Cloud when he was a boy. Red Cloud was learning how true this is. The joy of growing up with his free and well-living and friendly people had now moved around the circle to the pain of his grown-up years.

So his years were spent leading a people whom the white people were trying to buy off. A people who could no longer trust as openly as they had. A people who must always be on guard.

The Lakota ideas of sharing, bravery for the people, union with all that is, and individual freedom must live. The people must live. The joy of the people in their united ways of life, which no one could crush, were the only joys they had left now.

Great leaders such as Crazy Horse, Sitting Bull, Gall, Spotted Tail, American Horse, and Red Cloud all served in their own way, giving the best they had. They all served to give the children a future and their way of life a chance to survive.

And so Red Cloud used his words and his wit over and over and over. For these people who lived in their rich squares did not hear very well.

It was hoped that the pomp and power of Washington, D. C., that May, 1870, would impress Red Cloud. But so unmoved was he that he insisted on seeing the white leaders instead of the sights. Red Cloud insisted on speaking his mind about the type of white people the Great White Father sent west. The military, the treaty commissioners, and the agents. It is from these people that the Lakota got their image of white people. The image was not a good one.

There had been some well-meaning officers and soldiers. But many of the military officers were Indian-haters out to pick a fight and gain higher rank. During the Civil War, many of the soldiers sent west had been of the most undesirable character. Short of men, the military being engaged in the Civil War, ruffians were engaged for western duty.

Most of the treaty commissioners sent west did not take pains to consider the tribal system of the Lakota. The Lakota were in the habit of taking part in decisions. But tribes were not given fair choices. Nor were the treaties fully explained. The commissioners pushed "cracker and molasses" treaties. Feasts were given in exchange for sale of a Mother Earth the Indian people had never thought of buying and selling.

And now the Indian agents had begun to move in. The pay for Indian agents was low and it was a thankless job. There were not many applicants willing and able and of the moral fiber to do a decent job. Before long the government was having to investigate the agents.

Also needing investigation were the suppliers and transporters of the food and supplies to the reservations.

Red Cloud had not gone to Washington for sightseeing. During one conference he listened carefully and then it was time to speak. He shook hands with the officials with seriousness and said, "I came from where the sun sets. You were raised on a chair; I want to sit where the sun sets." He then sat down on the floor and delivered his reply.

Red Cloud (seated, wearing war bonnet) with a group of friends.
From the collections of the Library of Congress.

"I have offered my prayers to the Great Spirit so I could come here safe. Look at me. I was a warrior on this land where the sun rises, now I come from where the sun sets. Whose voice was first sounded on this land — the red people with bows and arrows. The Great Father (the President) says he is good and kind to us. I can't see it. I am good to his white people. From the word sent me I have come all the way to this house. My face is red, yours is white. The Great Spirit taught you to read and write but not me. I have not learned. I came here to tell my Great Father what I do not like in my country. The men he sends there have no sense, no heart. What has been done in my country, I do not want, do not ask for it. White people going through my country. Father, have you or any of your friends here got children? Do you want to raise them? Look at me. I come here with all these young men. All are married, have children, and want to raise them.

"The white children have surrounded me and have left me nothing but an island. When we first had this land we were strong, now we are melting like snow on the hillside while you are growing like spring grass.

"Now I have come to my Great Father's house, see if I leave any blood in his land when I leave. Tell the Great Father to move Fort Fetterman away and we will have no more troubles. I have two mountains in that country (Black Hills and Big Horn Mountains). I want Great Father to make no roads through.

"I have told these things three times now. I have come here to tell them the fourth time.

"I don't want my reservation on the Missouri. This is the fourth time I have said no. Here are some people from Missouri now. Our children are dying off like sheep. The country does not suit them . . .

"The railroad passing through my country now. I have received no pay for the land . . ."

Red Cloud, said New York newspapers, made something very clear. Avoiding telling the truth to the Indians doesn't work. Trying to jolly them or scare them doesn't work. Officials had better begin to talk straight.

Among Red Cloud's demands were that he choose where, on the reservation land, the agency would be. At the agency the supplies, which his people had given up much life-giving hunting ground to receive, were given out. And he had a continual fight to keep pinch-penny Congresses from decreasing the treaty supply amounts. And Red Cloud asked to name an agent from the people he knew and trusted.

But these kinds of demands had to be made over and over. The man must have grown tired of trips to Washington. His alert ears must have found it almost too much to have to listen to threats of removal to Indian Territory (Oklahoma). The watchful eyes must have often been clouded with hate, though his manner was usually strong and dignified before white people.

It was a continual and bitter fight. The battles were enough to crush a lesser leader.

The skins from the last buffalo hunts were worn now and the supplies issued for shelter were little protection against South Dakota winters. The proud Lakota were used to living well and eating much good meat when they were free to hunt. Now they were confined like prisoners. Mistrust resulted and many ridiculed Red Cloud. Many returned to Sioux bands still holding out. But the white army was increasing its forces against them. The white people were determined to confine all the proud Lakota people to the reservations.

Then came the seeds, plows, and overalls. The few who would use them saw their plants burned by drought or eaten by grasshoppers.

The churches did not stop and learn of the Lakota union that is deeply religious. It is union with each other, with rock, tree, water, the Great Spirit. The churches moved into the reservations and soon began to destroy the spiritual leadership of a deeply religious people. They said the Indian must change to their religion. Now.

The schools were also used to make the Indian children into white children. Hair was cut. Long hair meant manhood to the Indian men. And one day Red Cloud found his own daughter scrubbing a floor with a white woman threatening her. Half the day the students labored in the fields, or scrubbing, cleaning and maintaining the boarding schools.

These were the payments promised in the Treaty of 1868.

During that first trip to Washington, Red Cloud had spoken of that treaty. By public demand he had gone to New York City before returning home. Again he spoke of the Treaty of 1868.

"We came to Washington to see our Great Father that peace might be continued. The Great Spirit that made us both wishes peace to be kept; we want to keep peace. Will you help us? In 1868 men came out and brought papers. We could not read them, and they did not tell us truly what was in them. We thought the treaty was to remove the forts, and that we should then cease from fighting. But they wanted to send us traders on the Missouri River. We did not want to go to the Missouri, but wanted traders where we were.

"When I reached Washington the Great Father explained to me what the treaty was, and showed me that the interpreters had deceived me. All I want is right and just. I have tried to get from the Great Father what is right and just. I have not altogether succeeded . . . We do not want riches, but we want to train our children right. Riches would do us no good . . . The riches that we have in this world, Secretary Cox said truly, we cannot take with us to the next world.

"Then I wish to know why the Commissioners are sent out to us who do nothing but rob us and get the riches of this world away from us? I was brought up among the traders, and those who came out there in the early times treated me well and I had a good time with them. But, by and by, the Great Father sent out a different kind of men; men who cheated and drank whisky; men who were so bad that the Great Father could not keep them at home and so sent them out there.

"I have sent a great many words to the Great Father but they never reached him. They were drowned on the way, and I was afraid the words I spoke lately to the Great Father would not reach you, so I came to speak to you myself; and now I am going away to my home."

The crowd applauded after almost every sentence and at the end the clapping thundered for some time.

As he went home he had won his first skirmish of battle by wit and word. He held a big key to peace or war, to life or death. He had not staggered under the load.

CHAPTER IV

Agents, Missionaries, Commissioners

On returning to his people, Red Cloud found the problems the same. Hunger, cold, sickness.

While Red Cloud's eyes were watching all of this, Red Cloud's ears were hearing that the Lakota were losing the Black Hills.

Paha Sapa. Sacred Land of Lakota prayers and fasts. They were told they must lose them because white people who were never to enter Indian land had entered. And found gold. Gold was the real God of far too many whites.

And so more promises and gifts went to the Lakota and the Black Hills went. Also lost over the years has been all but the spots on the North and South Dakota map. Spots of reservation land. And on that reservation land are white communities and white ranchers.

When Red Cloud grew up and became Itanca it was a hard time to be a leader. And an Indian does not become a leader to get fame for himself. He becomes a leader because his people need his ability.

Red Cloud knew his people did not believe in selling the Mother Earth which gave them life. And they always decided things in small groups. No one person could sell any-

The Black Hills — Needles in Cathedral Park,
near Custer City, South Dakota.
South Dakota State Historical Society.

thing that was part of them all. But the white people who seemed to be an endless, rushing powerful stream did not take time to learn. They used each other and Mother Earth, rather than unite with each other and Mother Earth.

The white people did not think of those who would come later. They wanted all the timber. All the gold. And their cities filled the rivers with waste. Because they saw only now. And themselves.

They were in a hurry. They could not take time for the Lakota people to decide their own future or to learn the closeness and happiness of a dignified people.

The Lakota had many groups or bands of people. Each had several leaders. There were leaders in battle, leaders in camp, leaders in the holy matters. All leaders served the people. Leaders carried out the wishes of the people. The white world would not take time to consult each band of the Lakota. So they named such leaders as Red Cloud the head of all the many Sioux bands.

This had not been done by the Lakota. They did not like it. No one man could speak for all of them. And, at that, the white people had no right to decide who that one person should be.

But the treaty commissioners did decide. And when they were through, the agents decided. Once they set up a leader they tried to get him to take orders. Such strong leaders as Red Cloud and Spotted Tail could lead the people even when the agents tried to break their power, but the agents had ways to force the people to follow the agents. An agent could cut off the supply of food. He could send for troops, or at least threaten to.

Little by little, the agents were often able to break down

the strong unity of the people following leaders of their own choice. The agent could rule better if it was every man for himself, rather than if all would stand together.

In regard to dividing the supplies (and at other times) Red Cloud often got his way and saw to the dividing. An old treaty had given the leaders chosen by the people this right. Red Cloud learned quickly to throw the white people's own tricks at them to help his people.

Not only did the agents attempt to destroy the leadership but the missionaries were equally to blame for the destruction of the spiritual leadership of the people. Agent and missionary often worked together to change the Indians to white ways with a complete disregard for thousands of years of Indian culture.

On Red Cloud's reservation the agents even decided which white religion the Indian people could be exposed to. When an Episcopalian was agent, he would allow no Catholic priests on the reservation. Then when a Catholic agent took over, he tried to stop the Lakota ceremonies.

The ceremonies and the holy men had kept the people on the good road of morality, generosity, sharing, and a complete involvement of oneness with *Wakan Tanka,* the Great Spirit.

The *wasicu* (non-Indian) came with his many squares of religion — Mormon, Catholic, Episcopal, Jehovah Witness, Church of Christ, and so on. Their struggle for Indian souls was bewildering to the captive reservation people.

The closeness and dependency upon the Great Spirit was stamped out through the boarding schools and missionaries. The holy men were ridiculed and many sacred bundles were destroyed. The Pine Ridge Reservation agent ordered the army to gather up the sacred bundles, pipe bags, tobacco pouches, and medicine kits. The people were then herded to watch the gathered pile of holy articles being soaked with oil. A match was touched, by a soldier, to the sacred bundles and peace pipes. Red Cloud with his Oglala people had to stand and watch their beauty burn, while the agent and the missionary looked on. The missionary was pleased with himself for taking part in this insensitive act because, after all, in his mind they were pagans for him to save.

The Lakota were told to worship God in square houses instead of in a sacred outdoor ceremony, or alone on a hill. But to the Lakota people, white religion was enclosed, stuffy, and in a foreign language.

This was a great contrast to the natural surroundings the Indian used. The Indian saw God all around him, in the God-made nature. Instead of seeking Wakan Tanka on a lonely hilltop (*Hanbleceya yapi*, vision quest) the Lakota were told to see the Father or Reverend. Instead of the huge tribal spiritual uniting of the Sun Dance, the Lakota were scattered piecemeal to the winds by the different Christian missionaries.

It was not just in Red Cloud's day that the attempted destruction of the roots of the Indian culture occurred. It still goes on. A Holy Man of Red Cloud's people was told in recent years he would have to give up his performing of a sacred Indian ceremony. To this day, the Catholic priest at Pine Ridge still stands by at the Sun Dance with his portable altar in the back of his pickup, ready to move into the base of the sacred tree to say his ceremony. He believes that the Indian ceremony is not a complete ceremony, yet when the Sun Dance was taught to the Indian people by the Great

Spirit no mention of change was instructed to the people, nor has further spiritual instruction been given. Never have the Indian people interfered with the holy services of the Christians.

It would not be true to say that the Lakota shut out the new religions. They had been so close to Mother Earth that they could see beauty and were very open to it. When the Spanish brought the horse, Indians quickly became some of the best horsemen in the world. And they adopted many of the inventions of the non-Indians. But they always wanted to choose to leave alone that which would be bad for the people. They wanted to pick up only that which would not destroy their true beliefs.

Where they saw beauty in the white religions, they accepted it. For they are a very religious people. But Red Cloud and others worked hard and risked much to keep the Lakota ways alive despite all the pressure to smother them.

The soldiers had not defeated Red Cloud, nor had the treaty commissioners. He would not allow un-Christlike priests and ministers to order him or his people around.

The Lakota are not a people given to bowing before anyone. Red Cloud and other leaders displayed this at the Black Hills Commission in 1875. The leaders were so firm that talk was stopped. Red Cloud had been specific:

"There have been six nations raised, and I am the seventh, and I want seven generations ahead to be fed . . . These hills out here to the northwest we look upon as the head chief of the land. My intention was that my children should depend on these hills for the future. I hoped that we should live that way always hereafter. That was my intention. I sit here under the treaty which was to extend for thirty years. I want to put the money that we get for the Black Hills at interest among the whites, to buy with the interest wagons and cattle. We have much small game yet that we depend on for the future, only I want the Great Father to buy guns and ammunition with the interest so we can shoot the game.

"For seven generations to come I want our Great Father to give us Texan steers for our meat. I want the Government to issue for me hereafter, flour and coffee, and sugar and tea, and bacon, the very best kind, and cracked corn and beans, and rice and dried apples, and saleratus [baking soda] and tobacco, and soap and salt, and pepper, for the old people.

"I want a wagon, a light wagon with a span of horses, and six yoke of working cattle for my people. I want a sow and a boar, and a cow and bull, and a sheep and a ram, and a hen and a cock, for each family.

"I am an Indian, but you try to make a white man out of me.

"I want some white men's houses at this agency to be built for the Indians. I have been into white people's houses, and I have seen nice black bedsteads and chairs, and I want that kind of furniture given to my people . . .

"I want the Great Father to furnish me a sawmill which I may call my own. I want a mower and a scythe for my people. Maybe you white people think that I ask too much from the Government, but I think those hills extend clear to the sky — maybe they go above the sky, and that is the reason I ask for so much . . ."

The Commission of 1875 disbanded. The Lakota leaders would not give in. The Commissioners would not meet their demands. The Black Hills still were Lakota.

One year later they were gone. In a quick flash the Black Hills were gone. And much other Indian land went with it.

This time the Commissioners completely ignored Article 12 of the Treaty of 1868. At least three-fourths of all adult male Indians must sign any cession of any part of the reservation. The commission settled for signatures from the chiefs and two head men of each tribe.

Those who signed, including Red Cloud, were under pressure of threats to have rations cut off from the people. They were left confused about what they were signing. The mood

Red Cloud's home at the Pine Ridge Agency.
South Dakota State Historical Society.

of the white people had forced the issue, and the Lakota were presented a final demand. Supplies would be cut off unless they signed.

Part of this signing was agreement of a move to the hated Missouri River lowland or else to Indian Territory. So Red Cloud made more trips to Washington to avoid this.

Red Cloud said to the President, in part:

"There is a rumor of somebody going to the Missouri River. I wish you would not mention that to me; for I do not want to go on the Missouri River. The Missouri River is the whiskey road and if I went there I would not do good; I would come to nothing at all.

"West of where I am I could raise everything, good grass, fine country for stock, while on the Missouri River I do not see that I could raise anything, and the people there would ask a big price for their stock and would try to get all the advantages they could from me.

"Another thing, in the winter the river would freeze up and then I could get help from no one. The railroad goes very near where I am now, and I think since the road has been there I have been doing very well; I am not poor; I live very well."

The next morning when conferences continued he spoke more of what he wanted. A Lakota leader speaking of what he wants is really speaking of and for his people. He stands as a symbol for their needs and wants when he speaks of "I."

". . . now that I have got to be civilized I want to select a country for my Nation, and that is what I want to say to you today . . .

"Tongue River has four forks, but down by the prairie there is a good place to put an Agency, and there is where I want my Agency. I did not come here to give you anything. The Black Hills is my country, but I gave it to the commissioners, and sent word down here.

"Suppose you decide now what you are going to give me for the Black Hills. I came here to get it.

"I want three different kinds of wagons to work with . . . I want plows and moving machines. I will not say how many I want, but I want enough for my people. The cattle I want you to give me so that we can raise cattle, and raise them every year.

"I want two mills, but one is to saw wood with and the other to grind corn . . .

"I want you to give me school teachers, so that we will have a good school house, and teach my children how to write and read.

"That agent (Irwin) is the one I want."

When the Tongue River site was denied, Red Cloud asked for a White Clay River site. He finally won out in the end. However, the name was changed from Red Cloud Agency to Pine Ridge Agency. Too many people had felt the sting of Red Cloud's wit and words. To this day the Oglala people have the Pine Ridge name for their reservation.

CHAPTER V

Last
Years

With the question of the agency site settled, it was time for a new crisis to test Red Cloud. He was now almost sixty. Irwin had been agent but had resigned. And before long, Red Cloud needed to put pressure on Washington again. They had sent another of the agents who rule rather than help the people.

So after two years of battling with the agent, V. T. McGillicuddy, Red Cloud sent a letter to President James Garfield. He threatened that unless the President removed the agent he would do so.

A copy of the letter got back to McGillicuddy.

Red Cloud was called into a meeting room crowded with fellow Lakota. The meeting was led by McGillicuddy. The following is part of a report to the Nebraska State Historical Society which said the meeting went like this:

"Red Cloud, stand up."

The old chief sneered.

"Red Cloud, stand up. Red Cloud I have been your agent for three years. I have never lied to you. I have never promised you anything and failed to perform. I have sent the soldiers away so that they might not annoy you. There is not a soldier within sixty-six miles of this agency.

*The Pine Ridge Agency and Soldier's Camp
at the time of the Sioux War, 1890.*
South Dakota State Historical Society.

"Red Cloud, you have been mean and insolent. You have defied your agent and insulted the Great Father by sending him this letter.

"Because you have been mean and insolent, because you have defied your agent and insulted the Great Father I now break you of your chieftainship. You are no longer Chief of the Oglala.

"Man Afraid, I make you chief of the Smoke Band. American Horse, you are chief of the Bear Band. Red Cloud, to your tipi."

It was a dramatic moment. The two men stood face to face, each looking deep into the eyes of the other. The Oglala nation sat breathless upon the issue.

Presently Red Cloud's eyes fell. "To your tipi," repeated McGillicuddy with a gesture of dismissal.

This is what the report said.

McGillicuddy had to keep breaking Red Cloud's power over and over, though. The Oglala people kept going to him for leadership, as they always had.

"Red Cloud, to your tipi."

According to this story, Red Cloud who was nearing sixty, and had risked his life for his people, was shamed. In this case who looks to be the greater man? The man with the force of cannons behind him or the one with nothing but the example of a hard life lived for his people?

Sometimes apparent defeat turns into victory in the end. Good people and good ideas cannot be crushed. If this is true, and the Lakota people and ideas were good, then the last hundred years of crushing has not worked.

White people judge by victory they can see right now. The Lakota people see the big picture. Of union with all that is. Of happiness and the working together of all that is.

In that picture, with which people lies victory?

It is clear that all white people were not as blind to ultimate truth as McGillicuddy. The report of the commissioners who finally took the Black Hills includes these words:

". . . . If we sow broken faith, injustice and wrong, we shall reap in the future as we have reaped in the past, a harvest of sorrow and blood. We are not simply dealing with a poor perishing race; we are dealing with God.

"We cannot afford to delay longer fulfilling our bounden duty to those from whom we have taken that country, the possession of which has placed us in the forefront of the nations of the earth.

"We make it our boast that our country is the home of the oppressed of all lands. Dare we forget that there are also those whom we have made homeless, and to whom we are bound to give protection and care?

"A great crisis has arisen in Indian affairs. The wrongs of the Indians are admitted by all. Thousands of the best men in the land feel keenly the nation's shame. They look to Congress for redress. Unless immediate and appropriate legislation is made for the protection and government of the Indians, they must perish. Our country must forever bear the disgrace and suffer the retribution of its wrong-doing. Our children's children will tell the sad story in hushed tones, and wonder how their fathers dare so to trample on justice and trifle with God . . . . ."

The treaty commissioners who wrote this must not have been able to sleep well. What they had proposed to the Lakota chiefs had been such a sour dose that Sitting Bull had left in an outrage.

Those chiefs who did sign were told there would be a feast afterwards. It was a very solemn feast. Crow refused to sign. Fire Thunder held his blanket over his eyes while he signed. Almost every chief who signed made a speech. The words indicated they did not understand the treaty. The words indicated they would not abide by that which they did not understand or agree with.

Young-Man-Afraid said, "I give notice it will take me a long time to labor, and I expect the President will feed me for one hundred years, and perhaps a great deal longer."

"Civilizing" the Indians by making them into white people was strongly written into the treaty. Industry, education, and white morality were the Gods of the white people. So they must be the Gods of the Indians. To this day the schools to which the Indian children must go teach white values. This causes a conflict in children who were taught by their grandparents to be Indian. So about half the children drop out of school because of the struggle going on in them.

In 1897, the seventy-five year old chief made his last trip to Washington. He complained about the judges of the Indian courts on the reservations. He said they fined everyone and no one knew what happened to the money the people paid to them. He thought the courts should be abolished.

And in 1903, the eighty-one year old man spoke at his last talk to the Pine Ridge council. He was still angered by the stealing of the Black Hills in 1876.

"Quite a while ago I used some words with the Great Father. It must have been twenty-six or twenty-eight years ago and I have missed most of the words. There was a man

Red Cloud as photographed by David F. Barry, date not recorded.
Smithsonian Office of Anthropology, Bureau of American Ethnology Collection.

came from the Great Father who told me, 'Red Cloud, the Great Father told me to come and see you. So the Great Father told me to come to you because he wants the Black Hills from you.' So I asked, 'How much money did you bring for the Black Hills?' He answered me, 'I brought six million dollars.' So I answered him, 'That is a little bit of a thing.' I told him like this, 'The Black Hills is worth to me seven generations, but you give me this word of six million dollars. It is just a little spit out of my mouth.' Then he said, 'Let me have the Black Hills and the Big Horn both together.' But I told him this, 'That is too small; so I won't do it.' And I kept this land. 'So you can go back to the Great Father and say that to me the Black Hills is worth seven generations.'

" 'You can tell the Great Father that I will lend him the top of the hills, if he is satisfied, that is what you can tell him. That is just the rocks above the pines.' I would like to tell you this my friend; the rations they give us only last for a day. They should give us the money from the Black Hills treaty, because we need it now. I have been to Washington fifteen times and this is something like the making of a treaty . . . ."

Red Cloud lived mostly in retirement his last years. He had trouble with his eyes. He would visit the Shoshoni reservation and bathe in the warm springs. On one of the trips, in July, 1894, this man who had once roamed with his people over the entire area, was put in jail and fined for killing game out of season. If it is possible to look at the good side of this we could ask how many men of seventy-two with bad eyesight could hunt with results.

Red Cloud and his wife often went to Nebraska to camp

on the Niobrara River, a shaded area much different from the heat of the nearly treeless agency in South Dakota. He had friends who welcomed him to their ranch to talk over old times, the Captain James H. Cook family. His last visit, in 1908 at the age of eighty-six, lasted ten days.

As he neared death he must have watched his people carefully with their broken circle and lack of leaders. On July 4, 1903, Red Cloud formally gave his chieftainship to his son Jack. The Sioux did not depend on bloodlines for leaders. Each person must prove his ability to lead. But the gesture had once been made for Red Cloud so he made it for his son Jack.

But the agents had worked hard to break the power of the chiefs. They had wanted that power. So in years ahead many people were given the chief title to keep them in good humor, even though the title was often empty.

Even today, however, the Indian people have those quiet men in the background who talk little but are very wise. To these Indian leaders the people still go. They may not be seen in tribal councils, but they are there. Tribal councils today often are yes-men to the agents, but times are changing. New tribal council members, especially those who respect and keep the deep culture and traditions, are emerging. The agencies are finally losing their powers and the Indian people have some voice in their own government, but many barriers are still before the people.

But just as Red Cloud was strong long after he was "broken" by the agent, so there are men today who lead from the simple position of the respect of their people.

Red Cloud was an old man at the time another of the Oglala band of Lakota, Black Elk, received a vision. The Lakota will have four generations that are very hard, the vision said. The road of poverty and despair will almost seem to take away their spirit. But during the fifth generation, the spirit will return and the people will again begin to walk the good road.

It seems that the vision came true. The poverty and the despair of the Lakota is still very real. The holy tree has seemed to be dying as hunger and cold and a new culture were forced on the people.

But the fifth generation is now beginning to walk among the people of Red Cloud. And during the years on the road of pain, the Indian ways did not die. Now they are coming to life again and they, like a holy tree, can shade people of other races. Black, yellow, white, and red.

For when a people are the carriers of a truth, they cannot have that truth crushed from them. Certainly the ways of acting brave for the people are different now.

Certainly sharing now means something different than giving the best meat of the hunt to the old and those unable to hunt for themselves. Now it means giving the things of this century, which Mother Earth also placed here.

Certainly individual freedom means choosing right for the people in a new setting. It means freedom to decide whether to go to college, whether to serve the people as a politician, doctor, soldier, or holy man — as well as still serving as Sun Dancer, dancer, drummer, singer, or viewer in the still beautiful powwows.

And today, adjustment to nature, being part of all that is, seems different in a jet age, a space age.

But the Indian ideas are still great today. They are timeless, and belong to all people in every age. The white people took almost all the Indian people had — buffalo, land, hunting grounds, sacred stone for their sacred pipes. For many years white people tried to stamp out Indian language and beliefs.

But the Indians stood the test and are now able to give the world the one thing they have left. The people of Red Cloud are ready again, in this fifth generation, to give their example.

The world needs the example of a people who are brave and can do a hard thing "so that the people will live." A people are needed who are sharing the best with those who are helpless. A people are needed who choose freely in the ways of living as a part of all, Mother Earth, each other, the Holy Ones.

And although the people are hungry, and some of them are bitter about all that has been taken, some are very ready to take this great Indian way and share it with their fellow Indian brother who also is hungry for the old beauty.

Red Cloud was old, about eighty-seven, when he died in his Pine Ridge, South Dakota home, December 10, 1909.

There will rise other leaders who can speak the truth to a world that still does not hear very well. Those who seem to win the things of the world are often the losers in the big picture of life and happiness. The Lakota see a bigger picture. In a world torn by people who cannot get along, from which people will come hope?

Yes, new leaders will rise among the people of Red Cloud. As he did they will speak the straight talk to a world that still does not hear very well. And the circle will have gone around. It will return to the good place.

And once again the drums will beat like the heartbeat of

a happy people who leave their tipis and join the moving circle of dancers.

And then a child's eyes will again see that the whole world seems to move in this circle of the people.

Monument in honor of Red Cloud.
South Dakota State Historical Society.

CHAPTER VI

Fifth
Generation

It was the first weekend in August, 1969; the young
Oglala warrior who was selected by his people to take part
in the beautiful *Wi-Wan Yang-Wa-Chi-pi* (Sun Dance)
stood near the center of the circle. He wore the ankle length
Sun Dance kilt, with red, black, yellow and white streamers
attached to it, and a sage crown formed a band around his
black hair. He was pierced through the skin of his chest with
a small wooden peg and he leaned back on the rawhide rope
connecting him to the sacred cottonwood tree at the very
center of the circle.

This Oglala's name was *Wanblee Wi-cha-sha* (Eagle
Man). He had taken the Sun Dance vow at Fools Crows
cabin during a Yuwipi spirit ceremony, held for him by the
old Sioux Holy Man to protect Eagle Man for his combat
assignment in faraway Vietnam. Now he was home, after
having flown 110 combat missions as a Marine pilot of a
Phantom jet fighter. All the predictions that the old holy
man made for the young warrior had come true and now he
must fulfill his vow to be pierced and to always live for the
people. He would now give his pain with other fellow
Lakota-Dakotas (Siouxs): Fools Crow, Eagle Feather,

Catches, Red Bow, Fire, and Gap. The tribal chairperson, the chief of the Oglalas, looked on, proud of his gathered people and respectful of the sacred occasion.

Sitting near the east entrance of the Sun Dance circle in a beautiful buckskin dress, her long hair braided and bright eyes gleaming, was LuLu Red Cloud, the great granddaughter of Red Cloud. She attended the same university as Eagle Man. She had the leadership traits of the Red Clouds; while only a freshman in college, she almost single-handedly arranged for one hundred eastern South Dakota homes to open for orphaned and homeless children during the Christmas season. Now she encouraged the Sun Dancers to always be brave and to live only for the people and not themselves.

A sharp pain went through the Sun Dancer as the peg made a small tear in his chest and pulled free, the dancer nearly losing his balance as he pulled backward. The vow was fulfilled and the thousands of Indian people who had gathered for four days of Thanksgiving on the plains of South Dakota could now return and another year's circle would start anew.

The ceremony ended with the Sun Dancers assembled in a line as the crowd of appreciative black, red, and white brothers and sisters filed by to shake the hands of the Sun Dance participants, and also to touch the peace pipes that they held. The people were very happy. LuLu Red Cloud filed by and said, "This is a good day to live. You men have brought new life back to the people because you are doing what the Great Spirit has asked his red children to always do in his honor."

The young warrior Eagle Man (Wanblee Wi-cha-sha) kissed his sisters, brothers, and old mother good-bye and left the Sun Dance grounds now that it was completed and went away by himself to rest in the Black Hills, Paha Sapa. He returned after a few days to Pine Ridge and went straight to Red Cloud's grave in the lonely churchyard at Holy Rosary Mission where the great leader is buried. The young Sun Dancer looked down upon the European grave with its large cross symbol and said to Mahpiya Luta, "Grandfather (Red Cloud), thank you for keeping our ways alive and never giving in to the evilness of the bad ways. The power of the hoop is not broken, it is still very much alive, our beauty will never die! Grandfather, you must be lonely here in the white man's graveyard where they advertise your bones on a highway sign down below. You must be lonely for the Indian symbol on your resting place. Surely when you were buried the missionaries would not allow our sacred sign (which stands for the power of the hoop, the four directions, and four races of man coming together) to be placed on your grave. I am going to put the symbol on your grave. Grandfather, if you do not want it, let me know. They say you became a Christian. Like so many of our people, it was probably easier for you to simply say 'Yes, I will become what you want,' only to end the badgering which the Indian people underwent many times at the hands of the agents and missionaries." (Many Indians became baptized several times in different faiths, to keep their government rations from being shut off, and to avoid social reprisal against their children in the boarding schools. The Indian people respected other religious ways but they never intended to give up their Indian ways.) Eagle Man brought forth his Sun Dance pipe and marked a red circle from the edge of the soft red catlinite peace pipe across the flat surface of the unnatural concrete vault. "There, Grandfather. Surely you must have been lonely for our way."

He then went into the town of Pine Ridge and met Lulu Red Cloud; they were going to return to the university that they both attended. Eagle Man told her what had taken place at the cemetery. "Good! Good!" Red Cloud's granddaughter's face lit up. "*LeLa Wasta,* it is real good."

THE AUTHOR

Born on the Pine Ridge Reservation in
South Dakota, which was Red Cloud's
home during his last years, Ed McGaa is a
member of the Oglala Sioux Tribe. Five
times he has been selected by the tribe to
serve as a Sun Dancer. McGaa is a
graduate of St. John's University in
Minnesota, and has a doctorate of
jurisprudence from the University of South
Dakota Law School. As a marine fighter
pilot, Captain McGaa flew 110 Vietnam
combat missions, and was awarded eight
air medals and two Vietnamese Crosses
of Gallantry. The former assistant director
of Indian education for the Minnesota
State Department of Education, he has
given numerous speeches throughout the
nation advocating Indian culture and
respect for Mother Earth. He is now
co-chairperson for the Minnesota
American Revolution Bicentennial and
Deputy Director of Human Rights for
St. Paul, Minnesota.

OTHER BIOGRAPHIES
IN THIS SERIES ARE

DUE DATE

MAR 23 1994			
JAN 31 1996			
JUN - 3 1996			
APR - 2 1997			
OCT 17 1997			
MAR 31 2003			
APR 26 2005			
JUN - 6 2007			

RULES

1. Books may be kept two weeks and may be renewed once for the same period.

2. A fine of five cents a day will be charged on each book which is not returned according to the above rule. No book will ae issued to any person incurring such a fine until it has been paid.

3. All injuries to books, beyond reasonable wear, and all losses shall be made good to the satisfaction of the Librarian.

4. Each borrower is held responsible for all books drawn on his card and for all fines accruing on the same.